S0-DQS-306

EXPLORING WORLD CULTURES

South Korea

Laura L. Sullivan

Cavendish Square

New York

Published in 2019 by Cavendish Square Publishing, LLC
243 5th Avenue, Suite 136, New York, NY 10016

Library of Congress Cataloging-in-Publication Data

Names: Sullivan, Laura L., 1974- author.
Title: South Korea / Laura L. Sullivan.
Description: New York : Cavendish Square, 2019. | Series: Exploring world cultures | Includes bibliographical references and index. | Audience: Grades 2-5.
Identifiers: LCCN 2017048057 (print) | LCCN 2017052110 (ebook) | ISBN 9781502638144 (library bound) | ISBN 9781502638151 (pbk.) | ISBN 9781502638168 (6 pack) | ISBN 9781502638175 (ebook)
Subjects: LCSH: Korea (South)--Juvenile literature.
Classification: LCC DS902 (ebook) | LCC DS902 .S84 2019 (print) | DDC 951.95--dc23
LC record available at https://lccn.loc.gov/2017048057

Editorial Director: David McNamara
Editor: Jodyanne Benson
Copy Editor: Rebecca Rohan
Associate Art Director: Amy Greenan
Designer: Christina Shults
Production Coordinator: Karol Szymczuk
Photo Research: J8 Media

The photographs in this book are used by permission and through the courtesy of:
Cover, Bill Bachmann/Alamy Stock Photo; pp. 5, 20 Chung Sung-Jun/Getty Images; p. 6 Pavalena/Shutterstock.com; p. 7 Paul Brown/Alamy Stock Photo; p. 8 Purchase, Lila Acheson Wallace Gift, 1997, Metropolitan Museum of Art/Crystal Kui/File: MET 1997 34 22 O1 sf.jpg/Wikimedia Commons; p. 9 File: Maj. R.V. Spencer, UAF (Navy) U.S. Army Korea, Installation Management Command/Korean War Refugee With Baby.jpg/Wikimedia Commons; p. 10 Korea.net (http://www.korea.net) / Korean Culture and Information Service /File: Inauguration of Moon Jae-in 04.png/ Wikimedia Commons; p. 11 Dean Purcell/Getty Images; pp. 12, 18 Topic Images Inc./Getty Images; p. 13 Oskar Alexanderson (http://flickr.com/photos/39610980@N05)/File: Samsung headquarters.jpg/Wikimedia Commons; p. 14 by eimoberg (http://flickr.com/photos/eimoberg/)/File: Korea-Mountain-Jirisan-08.jpg /Wikimedia Commons; p. 15 VPC Animals Photo/Alamy Stock Photo; p. 16 Stephane Roussel/Alamy Stock Photo; p. 19 RunPhoto/DigitalVision/Getty Images; p. 21 Ed Jones/AFP/Getty Images; p. 22 Eiko Tsuchiya/Shutterstock.com; p. 24 ddol-mang (http://flickr.com/photos/ysjjhfox/)/File: Korean.dance-Taepyeongmu-01.jpg/Wikimedia Commons; p. 26 Multi-bits/Photolibrary/Getty Images; p. 27 With God/Shutterstock.com; p. 28 Jun Ohwada (http://flickr.com/photos/21733281@N00/File: Korean cuisine-Japchae-03.jpg/Wikimedia Commons; p. 29 Project Manhattan, own work/File: Hwangnam bread.jpg/Wikimedia Commons.

Printed in the United States of America

Contents

Introduction

Ready to learn about South Korea? South Korea is
in East Asia. You will find Japan across the sea. It
is also called the Republic of Korea. South Korea
is a peaceful and healthy land. It has a strong
economy. South Korea is known for its population.
Its population is over fifty-one million people!

The country has a long, rich history. However,
it has also suffered through war. South Korea is
divided from its neighbor, North Korea. The two
countries are very different.

South Korea has a strong government. It
also has a beautiful culture and great food. It
has four different seasons. You could find a hilly

countryside with cherry trees. You can also find old Buddhist temples. South Korea even has busy cities like Seoul, the capital, and islands. There is so much to explore in South Korea!

South Korea is an interesting country that has come a long way in a short time.

Geography

South Korea is the southern part of the Korean Peninsula. This peninsula borders China. South Korea's northern neighbor is North Korea.

A map of South Korea.

The country has many hills and low mountains. There are about three thousand small islands offshore. The Yellow Sea is to the west. The Sea of Japan is to the east. Japan lies to the

FACT!

The national flower is a hibiscus called *mugunghwa,* or "eternal flower."

south across the Korea Strait. Major rivers include the Nakdong, the Han, and the Geum. There are very few natural lakes, but many man-made ones.

The Han River flows through the capital city, Seoul.

Winters are cold and long, without much snow. Summers are short and humid. Sometimes there are typhoons, or huge tropical storms, in late summer or early fall.

The Big Divide

The **demilitarized zone** separates North from South Korea. No one goes there. It has turned into a wildlife sanctuary. There may be tigers and bears living there.

History

Humans first came to the Korean Peninsula about ten thousand years ago. For some of its early history, the region was divided into three kingdoms. The kingdoms were sometimes separate and sometimes unified. During the Joseon Dynasty (1392–1897), Korea was **isolationist**. That means it did not allow visitors or ideas from other countries to enter.

Early Korean pottery over 10,000 years old.

FACT!

Kim Dae-Jung was the South Korean president from 1998 to 2003. He won the Nobel Peace Prize in 2000 for trying to achieve peace and democracy.

"Goguryeo"

The name "Korea" comes from "Goguryeo." This is the name of one of the early kingdoms in what is now Korea.

From 1910 until the end of World War II (1939–1945), Korea was occupied by Japan. After the war ended, Korea was split into two countries. North Korea was influenced by the Soviet Union. South Korea

The Korean War was hard on the people of South Korea.

was influenced by the United States.

Later, each government claimed to control the entire peninsula. In 1950, North Korea invaded South Korea. The war ended in 1953. However, peace was never declared.

South Korea is a republic. This means that power is held by the country's voters. They elect people to represent them. Like the United States, South Korea has three branches of government. The executive

Moon Jae-In is the current president of South Korea.

branch is responsible for governing. The legislative branch makes the laws. The judicial branch decides how the laws apply to real cases.

   The president of South Korea is elected to a

FACT!

The official residence of the president is called the Blue House.

Separate from all branches of government is the National Human Rights Commission of Korea. It keeps its independence so it can better protect human rights.

single five-year term. He or she cannot serve a second term. The current president is Moon Jae-In. The president nominates a prime minister.

The Blue House is where the president lives.

The National Assembly, or the legislative branch, has to approve the choice. The prime minister acts something like a vice president would in the United States.

Seoul is the South Korean capital. It is the sixteenth-largest city in the world by population.

The Economy

South Korea has a very strong economy. It is the eleventh-largest economy in the world. It is also the fourth-largest economy in Asia.

Hyundai is a popular brand of car made in South Korea.

However, this wasn't always the case. When the Korean War ended, South Korea was one of the world's

FACT!

Korea's fast economic growth was named the "Miracle on the Han River" because of the river that runs through Seoul.

Tourism

Tourism is also a big industry. More than eleven million tourists visit South Korea each year.

poorest countries. Within one generation, though, their economy became very strong again. The country didn't have many natural resources. Instead, they relied on selling

This is the headquarters of Samsung.

manufactured goods to other countries.

Workers in South Korea are very educated and skilled. Electronics and cars are two of their biggest products. The car brands Hyundai and Kia are from South Korea. So are Samsung phones.

The Environment

South Korea's fast growth meant that the environment suffered at first. As cities grew, forests were cut down. Natural areas were polluted. However, South Koreans have recently realized the value of natural places.

Jirisan National Park is one of the largest nature preserves in South Korea.

Today, there are projects to restore and preserve some of those wild places.

South Korea gets 29 percent of its electricity from nuclear power.

The country also works to make everything green and energy-efficient. They are increasing use of renewable energy, like solar and wind energy. At the same time, they are reducing reliance on **fossil fuel**.

Even though South Korea is trying to reduce pollution, its neighbors make that difficult. China makes massive amounts of air pollution. Some of that drifts to South Korea. That can create acid rain, smog, and toxic dust storms.

The Asian black bear is a rare species in South Korea.

Water Safety

The tap water in Seoul recently became safe to drink. In other cities, though, many people boil or filter their water.

The People Today

There are more than fifty million people living in South Korea. A lot of people live in a small space. There are about 505 people for every square mile of land. Most people live in the big cities, like Seoul.

Seoul is a very crowded city with many apartments, stores, and restaurants.

Most people who live in South Korea are of Korean background. Recently, more workers from places like China have come into the country. There are also about 28,500 United States military members living in South Korea.

16

South Korean citizens tend to see themselves as a unified group working toward common goals. Almost all of the population shares a language, religion, and culture. Many South Koreans are very traditional in some ways. However, the country is also known for being a very strong leader in technology and entertainment.

Long Lives

The average life expectancy in South Korea is eighty-one years. By comparison, the average life expectancy in the United States is 78.7 years.

Lifestyle

South Koreans tend to have small families. For several decades, most families only had one child. The birth rate has recently begun to increase.

Most families only have one or two children.

In South Korean tradition, it is the son who carries on the family name. He is also expected to take care of his parents when they get old. So, some families stop having children if their firstborn is a boy.

Women are legally equal to men. Men and

Many South Korean children start kindergarten at age three.

College

About 80 percent of South Korean children who graduate from high school go to college. By comparison, about 70 percent of United States high school graduates go to college.

women get the same education. However, there is a tradition that men are supposed to work. Women are expected to raise the children.

Many women work outside of the home, but some stay home with their children.

Education is very important in South Korea. Children are pushed to succeed from a very early age. Many South Koreans attend college after high school.

South Korea has no official state religion. South Koreans can believe in any religion they want.

These monks are celebrating Buddha's birthday.

A little more than half of South Koreans aren't members of any church. Some South Koreans are atheists. This means that they do not believe in any god or religion. Others practice the original religion of South Korea. It is called Korean shamanism. About 27.6 percent of

FACT!

In Confucianism, there are rituals and prayers to honor ancestors.

the people are Christian. About 15.5 percent are Buddhists. There is also a small number of Muslims in South Korea.

Many South Koreans believe in the spirit world and shamanism.

Confucianism isn't really considered a religion in South Korea anymore. However, it is a part of the traditional culture. It focuses on family loyalty and obedience to authority.

Christian Missionaries

Many members of South Korea's Christian community go to other countries to act as **missionaries.** This means that they try to spread their religion. South Korea has the second-highest number of Christian missionaries, after the United States.

Language

Korean is the name of the
language spoken in both
South Korea and North
Korea. It is called hanguk-
eo ("Korean language")
or sometimes just uri-mal

The Korean language has a
very unique alphabet.

("our speech"). Korean is not closely related to any
other modern language. Around the world, more
than eighty million people speak Korean.

Korean grammar depends on the rank of the
speakers. The language uses **honorifics**. This

FACT!

Korean is one of the most difficult languages
for English speakers to learn.

Language Changes

After they were divided, North and South Korea started using slightly different pronunciation. But, they can still easily understand each other when they speak.

means there is a special grammar used when speaking to someone of higher rank. For example, honorifics are used when children speak to their parents. They are also used when students speak to their teachers.

A long time ago, Koreans used Chinese characters for their written language. Later, a unique alphabet was created to write the Korean language. This alphabet helped both rich and poor Koreans learn how to read.

Arts and Festivals

South Korean arts are
a mix of traditional and
modern. The country has
many kinds of traditional
music and dance.
Sometimes music, dance,
acting, and martial arts are
mixed in traditional mask
dramas. South Korean
traditional painting uses ink on paper and
features images of nature.

Traditional Korean dances use elaborate costumes and unique hair styles and makeup.

One of the best-known K-pop hits is Psy's "Gangnam Style."

However, South Korea is also an innovator in the arts. Korean pop music (K-pop) uses many musical influences from around the world. K-pop is very popular, even in other countries. South Korean television series are also very popular in other countries.

South Korea has many festivals. They feature dancing, singing, athletics, and traditional games. Among them are Korean New Year, the first full moon festival, and the harvest festival.

Pororo

One of the biggest things to come out of South Korea is Pororo. This little animated penguin is popular in one hundred fifty countries. Pororo and his friends teach lessons about kindness and good behavior.

Fun and Play

South Korea has several kinds of martial arts that are popular around the world. Tae kwon do is a dramatic kind of fighting with many high kicks. It became an Olympic sport in 2000. Hapkido and Taekkyeon are two other martial arts styles.

Tae kwon do is a Korean martial art.

The two most popular sports here are soccer (called football by South Koreans) and baseball. In soccer, the national team has been at every World

FACT!

Seoul hosted the 1988 Summer Olympics. The South Korean city of Pyeongchang will host the 2018 Winter Olympics.

Cup since the mid-1980s. In 2012, the country won the Olympic bronze medal for soccer. Many South Koreans also watch or participate in basketball, hockey, and golf.

Families love to get into nature. They spend a lot of free time walking, hiking, or fishing. Scuba diving is becoming more popular. There are even good skiing and snowboarding spots in South Korea.

Video games are a competitive activity in South Korea.

Video Games

Video game competitions, or eSports, are very popular in South Korea. A lot of children and adults also play video games for fun.

Food

South Korea used to be a farming-based country. So, most of its popular dishes are based on grains and vegetables. Rice, beans, barley, and hot peppers are very popular. Since there is such a long coastline, seafood is also widely eaten. Beef is the most prized meat. Chicken, pork, and dog are also eaten.

Noodle dishes are served at birthdays to bring long life and weddings to bring long love.

FACT!

Extra-spicy foods are served during the hottest thirty days of the year.

Some foods are associated with certain festivals, or birthdays. Seaweed soup is served at most birthdays. So are noodles, which symbolize long life.

Desserts made from rice and sweetened bean paste are common. Other desserts and snacks include yumilgwa (fried dough with fruit or spice) and suksil-gwa (cooked fruit with honey). They also eat flavored rice cakes called tteok.

Small cakes with sweet red bean paste are a popular treat.

Kimchi

Kimchi is a Korean dish that is known around the world. This dish of **fermented** vegetables is high in nutrients.

Glossary

Confucianism   A way of thinking taught by Confucius, which includes respect for family.

demilitarized zone   A border barrier that divides North Korea from South Korea.

fermented   A food that is acted on by bacteria or yeast to produce a sour, preserved kind of food.

fossil fuel   Fuel made from long-gone living organisms, such as coal or natural gas.

honorific   A title or form of grammar that shows someone's rank or age.

isolationist   Believing that a country should not get involved with other countries.

missionaries   People sent to teach religion and serve others in another country.

Find Out More

Books

Dalrymple, Lisa. *Cultural Traditions in South Korea*.
New York City, NY: Crabtree Publishing Company,
2016.

Perkins, Chloe. *Living in … South Korea*. New York
City, NY: Simon Spotlight, 2017.

Website

National Geographic Kids: South Korea

http://kids.nationalgeographic.com/explore/
countries/south-korea/#south-korea-market.jpg

Video

Learn Korean Holidays: Children's Day

https://www.youtube.com/watch?v=Bbjn49hGxy8

31

Index

About the Author

Laura L. Sullivan is the author of more than forty fiction and nonfiction books for children, including the fantasies *Under the Green Hill* and *Guardian of the Green Hill*. She lives in Florida.